Module 3: Critical Thin

Introduction

What is *critical thinking* in the academic sense? It means using careful analysis to accept or reject *knowledge claims*. (A knowledge claim is a statement such as 'Watching violent films makes children behave violently.') Competent critical thinkers have to be able to distinguish between fact and opinion and to evaluate their own, as well as other people's, academic work. They need argumentation skills in order to construct sound or strong arguments and recognise fallacious arguments. Critical thinkers must be aware of how language is used to manipulate arguments. Finally, they have to take into account bias when evaluating knowledge claims.

After completing this module, you should feel more confident supporting or challenging them where necessary.

Contents

1 What is critical thinking?

At the end of this unit, you will be able to:

- understand the difference between thinking and critical thinking
- recognise the difference between a fact and an opinion
- use a framework to evaluate arguments

Task 1 Thinking skills

1.1 Circle the odd one out and give a reason.

| plane | bird | rocket | (dog) |

Reason: *A dog can't fly.*

a.

| apple | carrot | strawberry | banana |

Reason: _____

b.

| gold | diamond | platinum | silver |

Reason: _____

c.

| three | eight | six | four |

Reason: _____

d.

| baseball | soccer | tennis | cooking |

Reason: _____

1.2 Complete the next item in each sequence.

	3	7	3	7	3	7	3	[7]
a.	n	s	u	l	n	☐		
b.	3	3	3	7	3	3	☐	
c.	1	2	3	5	8	13	☐	
d.	2	4	8	16	32	☐		
e.	a	b	e	f	i	j	m	☐
f.	2	4	7	11	16	22	☐	

1.3 Work with a partner to compare your answers, then discuss what steps you took to find them.

Task 2 Critical thinking skills

To answer Tasks 1.1 and 1.2, you compared items in a sequence and looked for patterns. These are two examples of thinking skills which you probably use every day, for example, to predict if your bus is likely to be next or to put your clothes away in the right places (e.g., socks in a drawer, shirts in a wardrobe, etc.). Critical thinking is, however, a little different from everyday thinking skills.

Generally, critical thinking is used to understand and evaluate arguments. It is not important whether you agree or disagree with the arguments. Rather, critical thinking requires you to recognise that an argument is a good one, even if you disagree with it, or that another is a bad one, even if you agree with its conclusions.

2.1 **Read the argument carefully.**

> English has become a global language for a number of reasons. From an historical perspective, it spread to many parts of the world when successive waves of English speakers migrated abroad from the UK. In terms of the language itself, it is relatively easy to learn with its vocabulary, which is borrowed from many languages, and its fairly simple grammar. The economic dominance of English-speaking countries for many centuries has also contributed to its status as a global language. Indeed, English is likely to remain the number one global language forever.

2.2 **Discuss the questions with a partner.**

   a. What does the writer of this argument want you to believe?

   b. How does the writer try to persuade you?

   c. What is the writer's conclusion?

   d. Is the writer's argument logical? Why/Why not?

Task 3 Facts or opinions?

'What a beautiful car!' 'It's got a powerful engine.'

In academic work, it is important to distinguish a fact from an opinion. A fact is a piece of information which can be checked and proved. Something is a fact if, for example, we can observe it, test it or check it against some evidence. In contrast, an opinion is something which someone thinks is true. Unlike a fact, an opinion cannot be proved. However, sometimes the distinction between a fact and an opinion is not clear to us because so many people share the same opinion. Equally, new evidence may disprove something which was once considered a fact.

3.1 **Read the statements. Which is a fact and which is an opinion? Compare your ideas with a partner's.**

English is a very easy language to learn.
English is spoken all over the world.

3.2 **Read another statement about English. Underline <u>facts</u> and <u>opinions</u>.**

<u>English is better than other languages</u> because it <u>has a bigger vocabulary than other languages</u>.

a. English has borrowed many words from a wide range of other languages. Examples include 'tycoon' from Japanese, 'verandah' from Hindi, 'opera' from Italian, 'slim' from Dutch and 'junta' from Spanish.

b. English is spoken in more countries than any other language.

c. English is the language of Shakespeare, so it is superior to other languages.

3.3 **Work with your partner. Choose one of the essay titles (a–d) and identify the knowledge claim which is being presented either directly or indirectly. This is what you should be discussing in the essay.**

Girls are better readers than boys. = *a directly stated knowledge claim*

If we don't do more to protect the environment, we are heading for disaster. = *an indirectly stated knowledge claim* ('We can do more to protect the environment.')

a. Decisions about the practice of cloning should be made by experts who understand the science that is involved, not by the general public. Discuss.

b. A vegetarian diet is better for your health than one based on meat eating. Discuss.

c. A knowledge of Economics is essential for historians. Discuss.

d. One of the causes of juvenile delinquency is a result of poor attachment from birth. What might other causes be?

Task 4 Questioning opinions

4.1   In small groups, discuss and write the questions you would need to pose in order to accept, reject or suspend judgement of the opinions you have identified in Task 3.3, and what things you would need to evaluate.

          Opinion: *Girls are better readers than boys.*

          Questions: *Are girls better readers than boys? What evidence is there for this opinion?*

          Evaluation: *What do we mean by 'better'?*

a.   Opinion: _____

      Questions: _____

      Evaluation: _____

b.   Opinion: _____

      Questions: _____

      Evaluation: _____

c.   Opinion: _____

      Questions: _____

      Evaluation: _____

d.   Opinion: _____

      Questions: _____

      Evaluation: _____

Task 5 A checklist for evaluating facts and opinions

5.1   When you are critically evaluating others' or your own work, ask yourself the following five questions. Complete the questions using the words in the box.

evidence	~~unbiased~~	viewpoints	concepts	reasoning

a.   Is the issue under discussion clearly stated in an _unbiased_ way?

b.   Is relevant _____, experience and/or information provided?

c.   Are key _____ defined as necessary?

d.   Is there a clear line of _____, leading to logical conclusions?

e.   Are alternative _____ presented?

Task 6 Putting evaluation into practice

6.1 Read the essay question and work with a partner to underline the opinion.

The artificial language Esperanto would be a more appropriate global language than English in the 21st century. Discuss.

6.2 With your partner, discuss how to evaluate the opinions you have identified. Write the questions you would need to ask.

_____

_____

_____

6.3 Read the essay and use the checklist to evaluate it.

☐ unbiased?

☐ evidence presented?

☐ reasoning used?

☐ terms defined?

☐ alternative viewpoints presented?

Make notes and then compare your ideas with your partner's.

Ludwig Lazarus Zamenhof

_____

_____

_____

_____

_____

_____

_____

_____

_____

_____

_____

The artificial language Esperanto would be a more appropriate global language than English in the 21st century. Discuss.

Esperanto, which remains one of the best-loved artificial languages to date, was invented by the brilliant Ludwig Lazarus Zamenhof in the late 19th century. Zamenhof, a multilingual who spoke Russian, Yiddish, Polish, Hebrew, Latin, Greek, French, German and English, set out to develop an easy-to-learn universal second language which could help bring about world peace (Crystal, 1987).

How can a language help to bring about world peace? When he constructed Esperanto, Zamenhof hoped it would become a universal second language. He based his new language on a number of Indo-European languages. Its sounds are from Slavic and its vocabulary comes from a mixture of languages, including Latin, French, Spanish and German (Wells, 1989). As a result, it is not associated with any one nationality and may be considered a truly international language.

Due to its international status, Esperanto is now widely spoken around the world. Although estimates vary widely, it is thought to have between 100,000 and 15,000,000 speakers. By the 1970s, over 60 countries had a national Esperanto association (Crystal, 1987). It is thus a global language.

Given that it is so easy to learn, Esperanto could rapidly overtake English as the global language of the 21st century. For example, in the mid-1960s, approximately 1,000,000 people in 74 countries signed a petition addressed to the United Nations in favour of Esperanto becoming an official international language (Auld, 1988). Although the United Nations eventually rejected this proposal, the petition is evidence of Esperanto's popularity.

In conclusion, Esperanto would clearly make a better global language than English in the future, as it does not belong to any one group of people and so its speakers are all equal. Moreover, Esperanto is a popular language, with speakers all over the world. This fact also makes it a better global language than English. Finally, Esperanto is a relatively new language compared with English. Arguably, Esperanto is the language of the future; English is the language of the past.

Bibliography

Auld, E. F. (1988). *Esperanto: The early struggle for recognition.* London: Smiths Press.
Crystal, D. (1987). *The Cambridge encyclopedia of language.* Cambridge: Cambridge University Press.
Wells, J. (1989). *Lingvistikaj aspektoj de Esperanto* [Linguistic aspects of Esperanto]. Rotterdam: UEA.

Reflect

How do you decide on the following?

a. What am I going to wear today?

b. What am I going to eat for lunch?

c. Which newspapers' opinions do I believe?

What is the difference between the thinking skills you employ in each case?

After completing this unit, would you make any changes to your thinking processes?

Recognising strong or sound arguments

At the end of this unit, you will be able to:

* identify parts of arguments
* understand the relationship between the parts of an argument

An argument can be divided into two parts: premises and a conclusion. Premises give evidence to support the conclusion. In some cases, the conclusion may not be directly stated, but it can be understood by the reader.

Task 1 Constructing an argument

1.1 Read the example argument. Underline the <u>premise</u> (*evidence*) and the <u>conclusion</u> (*what we decide is true, based on the evidence*) in the second argument.

<u>My tutor is always on time for her lessons</u>, but today she is ten minutes late, so <u>something must have happened to her!</u>

Global warming is definitely happening. I don't care what people say, but it was hotter this year than it has ever been.

1.2 What are the unspoken premises in the arguments?

a. You can't travel to Bhutan without a visa, so Ali is going to have problems if he intends to fly out there tomorrow.

_____

_____

b. I heard on the radio this morning that Western Region trains will be very disrupted tomorrow, so Natalia will be late for the interview.

_____

_____

1.3 What are the unspoken conclusions in the arguments?

a. The student candidate who best reflects mainstream opinion is very likely to win the next student election. The policies put forward by Sarah Rollings most closely match popular opinion.

_____

_____

b. The ban on smoking in public places will hit profits in cafés and bars. My cousin owns a large chain of bars.

_____

_____

Task 2 Recognising arguments

There are three types of arguments: *valid*, *sound* and *strong*.

2.1 **The following are examples of the three types of argument. Read the three examples and underline the <u>premises</u> and the <u>conclusions</u>.**

a. Some manufactured food products contain nuts. Harry is severely allergic to nuts. Therefore, he should avoid certain manufactured foods.

b. My aunt has sent me a cheque every year since I was five years old. Therefore, I expect to receive a cheque for my birthday this year, too.

c. All Chinese people are good cooks. Li Juan is Chinese so, as a consequence, she must be a good cook.

2.2 **Read the definitions of the three types of argument. Match the definitions (1–3) with the arguments (a–c) in Task 2.1. Work with a partner to check your answers.**

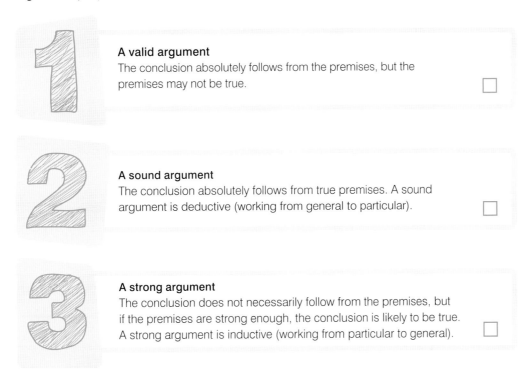

1 **A valid argument**
The conclusion absolutely follows from the premises, but the premises may not be true. ☐

2 **A sound argument**
The conclusion absolutely follows from true premises. A sound argument is deductive (working from general to particular). ☐

3 **A strong argument**
The conclusion does not necessarily follow from the premises, but if the premises are strong enough, the conclusion is likely to be true. A strong argument is inductive (working from particular to general). ☐

Note: *While it is good to be able to recognise a valid argument, you are more likely to use sound or strong arguments.*

Task 3 Checking your understanding

3.1 Match the types of argument (a–c) with the examples (1–3).

a.	A valid argument	1.	All dogs are black. Bingo is a dog, so Bingo must be black.
b.	A sound argument	2.	The food in this restaurant is always good, so we'll have a good meal today.
c.	A strong argument	3.	Brighton has a train station, so we can catch trains from Brighton.

3.2 Are the statements true (T) or false (F)?

a. Valid arguments are always good arguments. ☐

b. A sound argument can't have a false conclusion. ☐

c. If a strong argument has a false conclusion, then not all its premises can be true. ☐

3.3 Read five arguments from a seminar comparing the advantages and disadvantages of recruiting internally and externally. Decide if the arguments are valid, sound or strong. When you have finished, compare your answers with a partner's.

a. _____

> CANDIDATES RECRUITED INTERNALLY ARE THE BEST. SARAH WAS RECRUITED INTERNALLY, SO SHE MUST BE THE BEST.

b. _____

> Recruiting externally is more costly than recruiting internally. The cost differential is in the range of £1,000 plus.

c. _____

> Recruiting internally can cause resentment among staff. Employers should therefore provide counselling as necessary for those not selected.

d. _____

> Externally recruited employees bring with them expertise from their sector and as a result can be useful informants in their new workplace.

e. _____

> New employee induction programmes are not needed for internally recruited candidates. This saves the employer both the time and money spent on training externally recruited employees.

Task 4 Your examples

4.1 Find two examples of a sound argument based on your field of study.

_____

_____

_____

_____

4.2 Find two examples of a strong argument based on your field of study.

_____

_____

_____

_____

4.3 Work with a partner to compare your sound and strong arguments. Together, choose one sound and one strong argument. Copy them out onto a new piece of paper, but do not indicate which is which. Swap your arguments with another pair of students and see if they can identify the sound and the strong argument.

Reflect

'Sound and strong arguments are OK in academia, but not so useful in daily life.' Discuss. (100 words)

At the end of this unit, you will be able to:

* recognise weak arguments
* point out weak arguments politely

Task 1 Spotting fallacies in arguments

A *fallacy* is an argument where the conclusion does not naturally follow from the premises or is not likely to occur.

1.1 **Read the arguments and underline the <u>premises</u> and the <u>conclusions</u>. Work with a partner to discuss what is wrong with them as arguments.**

    a.   He hasn't replied, so he can't have received my letter.

    b.   He does not wear glasses, so he must have excellent eyesight.

    c.   English is superior to other languages and, as a result, is a global language.

    d.   I've double-checked my essay, so there can't be any mistakes in it.

Task 2 Poor argumentation strategies

There are certain strategies which can be used in place of proper argumentation. Four of the most common strategies are:

1. being subjective
2. appealing to common beliefs
3. invoking peer pressure
4. attempting to make others angry

2.1 **Match the strategies above (1–4) with the explanations (a–d).**

    a.   The speaker plays on your desire to conform and be the same as other people, but does not offer any premises or reasons why you should conform. ☐

    b.   The speaker tries to convince you of the validity of their opinion by making you annoyed rather than providing real evidence. ☐

    c.   The speaker does not examine the claim critically. Instead, they refer to their own experience. This is an attempt to stop any further discussion. ☐

    d.   The speaker encourages you to accept their argument by suggesting that most people believe it. ☐

2.2 Match the strategies (1–4) with the arguments (a–d).

a. ☐

GOVERNMENT TO WASTE MORE TAXPAYERS' MONEY

Our taxes are so high and the government is planning to use the extra revenue raised for opening multicultural centres. This is a complete waste of taxpayers' money.

b. ☐

URBAN LIVING CAUSES STRESS!

Everyone knows that living a rural life is preferable to the stresses of urban living.

c. ☐

FRUIT 'N' VEG BAD FOR YOU

The idea that we all need to eat five pieces of fruit or vegetables a day to be healthy may be true for some people, but it is definitely not true in my case.

d. ☐

POTTER MAGIC NOT WORKING FOR ADULTS

Harry Potter novels are childish and unsuitable for adults, so you should not read them.

2.3 Make changes to the arguments in Task 2.2 so that they are sound or strong.

a. _____
_____

b. _____
_____

c. _____
_____

d. _____
_____

Task 3 Checking your understanding

3.1 Read the excerpts (a–d) from a seminar on the advantages and disadvantages of urban living. Match them to the poor argumentation strategies (1–4) in Task 2.

a. People who live in the countryside are a bit strange. ☐

b. Listen, I know what I'm talking about. I've been living in a city for years, and I can tell you it is far more exciting than living in the suburbs. It's a fact. End of discussion. ☐

c. Building mega shopping malls in the suburbs is killing the heart of big cities. Doesn't it make your blood boil? ☐

d. Nobody thinks that living in a village is preferable to living in a city. Cities have everything you need – good quality healthcare and education as well as proper sanitation. ☐

3.2 In seminars, it is important to point out when someone is using poor argumentation. We often do this by using a negative question form and softening language, for example, *a little* + negative idea adjective.

Write a reply to the poor arguments in Task 3.1 using softening language.

a. _____

_____

b. _____

_____

c. _____

_____

d. _____

_____

Reflect

Find an argument between politicians on YouTube and analyse it for poor argumentation strategies. Show it to your class.

4 Persuasion through language or pressure

At the end of this unit, you will be able to:

- recognise when language, rather than reason, is used to persuade
- recognise when pressure, rather than reason, is used to persuade

Task 1 Making an idea sound better or worse

When we are talking about people fighting against a government, we can show our viewpoint by describing them as, for example, terrorists or freedom fighters. When we choose one of these descriptions, we are painting the fighters in a negative light (*terrorists*) or a positive light (*freedom fighters*). This choice of language indicates the speakers' attitude and may affect the listeners' viewpoint without them realising.

1.1 Write the words from the box in the correct column according to whether they have positive or negative connotations. They are all words and expressions that describe someone who is careful about spending money.

| stingy | economical | penny-pinching | mean | thrifty | tight-fisted | frugal |

positive connotations	negative connotations

1.2 A dictionary is a good place to find out if a word indicates a neutral, approving or disapproving attitude on the part of the speaker. For example, according to the Longman Dictionary of Contemporary English, a *cheapskate* is:

> **cheapskate** someone who spends as
> little money as possible – used to show
> disapproval *(informal): The cheapskate
> didn't even pay for the cab.*

1.3 Work with a partner to find positive and negative expressions for the following:

a. someone clever

_____

b. someone who talks a lot

_____

c. failing an exam

_____

Task 2 Making something sound less important or serious

When we *downplay* something, we try to make it seem less important or significant in order to advance our own argument.

2.1 **Rewrite the sentences to include the words or punctuation in brackets. Pay attention to the correct position in the sentence.**

a. He is a teacher. (*just*)

_____

b. It costs £20 a month to insure your life. (*a mere*)

_____

c. She got her degree from a university in the Midlands. (' ')

_____

2.2 **Work with a partner to discuss what each of the rewritten sentences means.**

Task 3 Making something seem more important or serious

Hyperbole is a huge overstatement which may be used to persuade people of our viewpoint. The strength of the overstatement may persuade us to believe what someone has said, even though they may not have given us any premises.

For example, *Mick Jagger is the most inventive musician who has ever lived*.

The use of hyperbole in this statement is designed to make the reader think Mick Jagger must be a very good musician (even if it does not make the reader think he is the most inventive musician who has ever lived).

3.1 **Work in small groups to discuss the hyperbole in the statements, and speculate why the speaker has used the hyperbole.**

a. 'I can't come to work because I am dying from a cold!'

b. 'My parents won't let me stay out later than midnight. They're such fascists.'

c. 'It's the most boring film in the world!'

3.2 **Write another example of hyperbole, then read your example to your group. Can the other group members decide why you used the hyperbole?**

'My mum makes the best apple pie in the world.'

Reason: To emphasise that your mum's apple pie is good.

_____

_____

Task 4 Pressuring the audience

Speakers and writers can push their audiences to agree by using pressure. They can suggest that:

1. all people would find their arguments logical and reasonable
2. all people who are like the listener/reader would find their arguments logical and reasonable

4.1 **Read the statements about marketing and decide which category (1 or 2) each belongs to.**

a. Anyone with half a brain knows that price is the most important factor for consumers.

b. An educated person understands how businesses try to convince consumers to buy their products.

c. It is universally acknowledged that red stimulates consumers to buy products.

d. Anyone can see that Flash jeans need to be promoted better if they are to survive.

e. All intelligent people recognise that function outweighs aesthetics when choosing a product.

Task 5 Using unreliable statistics

'There are lies, damned lies and statistics.' (Mark Twain)

We are often persuaded of the truth of an argument by the use of statistics, for example, *90% of women agree that this beauty cream reduces wrinkles in eight weeks*. What we may not know is that only ten women were asked, of whom nine agreed. Alternatively, these women may have been given generous gifts of the beauty cream as an incentive.

5.1 **Read the statements. What questions should we ask before we accept them?**

a. Eight out of ten dentists would recommend this toothpaste to their patients.

_____

_____

b. Only one in ten Americans possesses a passport.

_____

_____

c. We only use 10% of our brain! Just think what we'd be capable of if we could tap into the rest!

_____

_____

Task 6 Checking your understanding

6.1 Read the transcript of a discussion between two students about Esperanto and English. Underline the words and phrases they use to try to influence their listener unfairly.

A: Anyone with half a brain can see that Esperanto is an easier language to learn than English. It doesn't have any irregular verbs ... and it has the smallest vocabulary ever of any language.

B: But the 'language' of Esperanto is totally unknown. Who speaks it? No one.

A: Unknown?! It has slightly fewer speakers than English, but the difference in numbers is minimal.

B: You're joking! Esperanto only has a handful of speakers and there's a reason for that. It's OK for chit-chat, but you can't have a serious conversation in it.

A: Well, we're speaking English now and I wouldn't call this a serious conversation!

6.2 Compare your answers with a partner's. Discuss what happens to a discussion when language is used to persuade unfairly.

Reflect

'Language is a powerful tool for persuasion that can be used to good or bad effect.'
Discuss. (100 words)

5 Detecting bias

At the end of this unit, you will be able to:

* consider sources of bias in evidence in academic research
* identify possible reasons for researcher bias

A critical thinker must decide whether or not someone's point of view may have been affected by things such as personal agendas or vested interests. The critical thinker must ask him or herself questions about who has written a text or which organization might be funding the research.

Task 1 Detecting possible bias – Interviews

In some academic disciplines, interviews are used to collect evidence. These interviews can provide detailed information which is difficult to obtain from other sources. However, the information given by the interviewee may not be accurate.

1.1 **Work in small groups to answer the questions.**

    a.   Why might interviewees not give totally reliable information? Think about:

* the content of the questions
* the choice of vocabulary and language style
* the question types (*Wh~* or *Yes/No* questions)

    b.   An interview is an interaction between two or more people. How might the interviewer affect what the interviewee says? Think about differences in age, gender or culture.

    c.   What can the interviewer do to minimise his or her impact on the interviewee?

Task 2 Detecting possible bias – Researchers and sources of funding

The relationship between a researcher and the research, or the source of funding for the research, might also affect the findings.

2.1 **Work in small groups to discuss what possible bias might be involved in the following situations.**

    a.   A research report on the link between nicotine and Alzheimer's disease sponsored by the Tobacco Manufacturers' Association.

    b.   A study on student library use conducted by a library threatened with closure.

    c.   An ethnography of migrants living in Birmingham written by a British person.

    d.   A research report sponsored by a cereal manufacturer on the impact of fibre on a diet.

    e.   Analysis of a questionnaire on student satisfaction with a course, carried out by the course director.

2.2 **Work with a partner to discuss the questions.**

    a.   Think about the projects in Task 2.1. How could the researchers in these projects deal with the problem of bias?

    b.   What could a student do to find out whether a writer or source of information might be biased?

Task 3 Avoiding bias

Researchers are starting to reflect more on who they are and how their identity affects their beliefs and actions. They then share this information with their audience. This is known as *reflexivity*. Reflexivity has two benefits: it allows the reader to assess the work in question more easily, and it reduces the possibility of the writer being criticised for bias.

3.1 **Imagine you are going to write a report on how successful international students are at British universities. Should you inform your readers of any of the following information about yourself?**

☐ Your age   ☐ Your sponsorship (if any)

☐ Your religion   ☐ Your hobbies

☐ Your star sign   ☐ Your profession

☐ Your political affiliation   ☐ Your educational background

☐ Your nationality   ☐ _____

☐ Your weight   ☐ _____

☐ Your marital status   ☐ _____

☐ Your gender   ☐ _____

3.2 **Work with a partner to discuss any further elements to add to the list, and write your ideas above.**

3.3 **Using the elements you selected, write a brief description of yourself which outlines how your personal identity impacts on your practice.**

_____

_____

_____

_____

Reflect

'Is true objectivity ever possible?' Discuss in relation to your field of study. (100 words)

6 Putting it into practice: Taking part in a seminar

At the end of this unit, you will be able to:

- use your critical thinking skills to construct your own arguments
- evaluate your own and others' arguments using your critical thinking skills
- recognise different styles of arguing
- put together the skills you have developed in the earlier parts of the module

The outcome of this unit will be a discussion of the following question: *Can local cultures be preserved despite the globalisation of culture?*

Task 1 Understanding the question

1.1 Work in small groups to discuss the questions, making notes of your discussion.

    a. How can you define *culture*?

    b. What do you understand by the phrase *globalisation of culture*?

    c. What examples can you give of *local cultures*?

    d. What does the word *preserve* mean?

    e. What attitude towards culture does the word *preserve* suggest?

    f. What does the word *can* mean in the context of this essay title?

Task 2 Your view

It is important to be clear about your views on the discussion question.

2.1 Read the statements and mark a cross on each line to show how far you agree or disagree with them.

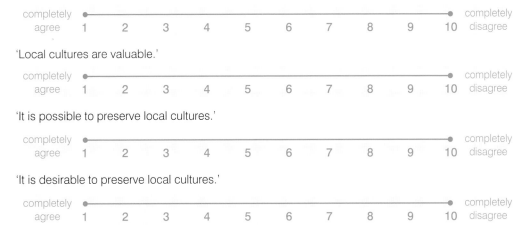

2.2 Work with a partner to compare your opinions. Give reasons for your opinions.

2.3 Work in small groups to discuss the questions.

    a. What are the alternatives to preserving local cultures?

    b. What would the consequences of these alternatives be in your opinion?

    c. Would these consequences be desirable? For whom?

Task 3 Gathering information

3.1 Work in small groups to discuss what questions you need to research in order to discuss the topic. Add them to the list.

- <u>How can globalisation be defined?</u>
- _____
- _____
- _____
- <u>What does cultural globalisation involve?</u>
- _____
- _____
- _____

3.2 Divide the research questions between the groups.

3.3 Read the Wikipedia article. Remember, you should not quote Wikipedia in any academic work, but it can be a useful starting point to find out about academic research done in the area. You should look at the sources in the References section at the end of the article and decide which of them are reliable, applying the criteria given in Unit 1, Task 5.

Share the following with the other members of your group:

- the information you have collected
- your evaluation of the arguments you have read

Cocacolonization

Cocacolonization (alternatively **coca-colonization**) is a term that refers to globalization or cultural colonization. It is a portmanteau of the name of the multinational soft drink maker Coca-Cola and the word *colonization*.

The term is used to imply either the importation of Western (particularly American) goods or an infusion of Western and especially American cultural values that competes with the local culture. [1] Whilst it is possible to use the term benignly, it has been used pejoratively to liken globalization to Westernization or Americanization. For example, according to linguist Ghil'ad Zuckermann, 'with globalization, homogenization and coca-colonization, there will be more and more groups added to the forlorn club of the lost-heritage peoples.' [2]

Marketing significance

Many governments attempt to resist the proliferation of American culture, usually by imposing quotas. For example, France was granted a cultural exception during the GATT negotiations, despite the objections of the American movie industry; as a result, in 2005, its domestic film market consisted of only 75% of US-originated content in comparison with 90% share of the other European countries. Canada also resorts to cultural protectionism, requiring a minimum share of Canadian content in domestic media. Many countries impose 'screen quotas' to protect their domestic film production, a practice started in the United Kingdom in 1927; other countries with screen quotas include France, South Korea, Brazil, Pakistan, Italy and Spain.

In October 2005, UNESCO's Convention on the Protection and Promotion of the Diversity of Cultural Expressions enshrined cultural exception as a method of protecting local cultures. Sponsored by France and Canada, the convention was passed 185-2, with four nations abstaining from voting. The notable naysayers were the United States and Japan. The United States claims that cultural exception is a form of protectionism that harms global trade.

References
Melnick, Merrill J., & Jackson, Steven J. (September 2002). 'Globalization American-style and Reference Idol Selection'. *International Review for the Sociology of Sport* 37 (3–4): 429-448. Doi: 10.1177/1012690202037004027
Ghil'ad Zuckermann, 'Sleeping beauties awake', *Times Higher Education*, January 19, 2012.
'Foreign News: The Pause That Arouses'. *Time*. 1950-03-13.
'BeWildered Berlin'. *Time*. December 8, 1961. Retrieved 2011-09-11.
Fabricating the absolute fake … – Google Books
Colossus: the price of America's empire – Google Books
Leatherman, T; Goodman, A (2005). 'Coca-colonization of diets in the Yucatan'. *Social Science & Medicine* 61 (4): 833–46. Doi: 10.1016/j.socscimed.2004.08/047.
Zimmet, P. (2000). 'Globalization, coca-colonization and the chronic disease epidemic: can the Doomsday scenario be averted?' *Journal of Internal Medicine* 247 (3): 301–10. Doi: 10.1046/j.1365-2796.2000.00625.x. PMID 10762445.
Kuisel, Richard F., (1991). 'Coca-Cola and the Cold War: The French Face Americanization, 1948–1953'. *French Historical Studies* 17 (1): 96–116. doi: 10.2307/286280. JSTOR 286280.
SPIN – Google Books
http://www.bbc.co.uk/iplayer/episode/b011llvt/Secrets_of_the_Superbrands_Food/
Cross-cultural marketing: theory … – Google

Task 4 Developing your argument(s)

You are now going to prepare for the final discussion. It is important to develop your argument(s) so that the discussion helps you to broaden your understanding of the issue, rather than just exchanging opinions. To do this, you need to be clear about your general argument and the more specific arguments which support it. It also helps to be aware of how an argument might be countered. This helps to strengthen your argument and prepare your defence.

4.1 **To think about your general argument, put a cross on the line below to show where you stand on this issue.**

'Local cultures can be preserved despite the globalisation of culture.'

completely agree										completely disagree
	1	2	3	4	5	6	7	8	9	10

4.2 **Think about arguments in support of the statement in Task 4.1 and complete Table A. Then think of counter-arguments against the statement and complete Table B.**

Table A: Arguments *in support* of statement

argument	supporting reason	example

Table B: Counter-arguments (*against* the statement)

argument	supporting reason	example

4.3 **Work with a partner. Take it in turns to explain one of your specific arguments with supporting reasons and an example. The other listens and then gives a counter-argument with supporting reasons and an example.**

Check:

• Do the premises support the conclusions in the specific arguments?

• Do the specific arguments support the main argument in turn?

Give your partner feedback in a helpful and supportive way.

Task 5 The seminar

5.1 Discuss the question in a seminar group, making notes of the arguments put forward by the various speakers.

Reflect

1. **Work in groups of three or four. Use your notes from the seminar to answer the questions.**
   a. Which three arguments that you heard in the seminar were most persuasive, and why?
   b. Which three arguments were least persuasive, and why?
   c. Did participating in the seminar change your overall opinion?
2. **Now work in a new group of three or four. Discuss the questions.**
   a. Did the speaker use positive or negative words? (Look at Unit 4, Task 1.)
   b. Did the speaker downplay something? (Look at Unit 4, Task 2.)
   c. Did the speaker overstate something? (Look at Unit 4, Task 3.)
   d. Did you feel the speaker was trying to pressure you into agreeing with him or her? (Look at Unit 4, Task 4.)
3. **Finally, discuss with a partner what you learned from participating in the seminar.**

Web work

Website 1

Critical discussions

http://www.criticalthinking.org

Review

This website provides an excellent discussion of definitions of critical thinking, articles to read and various other resources.

Task

Go to the website and search for the article *Learning the art of critical thinking*. Look at the list of statements called *How-to list for dysfunctional living*. How many of these statements could apply to you? How can your study of critical thinking help you to change some of those statements?

Website 2

Critical thinking quiz

http://www.cof.orst.edu/cof/teach/for442/quizzes/q1003.htm

Review

This site takes the form of a fun quiz which should inspire you to think critically. A discussion of the answers is also provided.

Task

Using the quiz as a model, create three questions of your own which also require critical thinking. Try these questions out on a fellow student.

Extension activities

Choose from the resolutions (a–d) and conduct in-class debates where different groups take it in turns to support or refute the resolution in question. The audience should vote on which team has carried the resolution.

a.   It is better to work for a small company than a large corporation.

b.   Foreign holidays are preferable to holidaying in one's home country.

c.   All undergraduate students should be required to live in a hall of residence throughout their time at university.

d.   Voting should be compulsory.

When you are planning your arguments, bear in mind the exercises you have completed on what makes a good argument and avoid the pitfalls of poor argumentation.

Activity 2

Find an essay you have recently submitted and analyse it using the checklist from Unit 1.

Activity 3

Listen to an episode of the BBC radio show 'Any Questions?'. Note any examples of speakers trying to persuade the audience by using positive or negative expressions, downplaying or overstating a point, or using statistics.

You can listen via the BBC iPlayer. You can also find a podcast of the most recent programme on the BBC website:

http://www.bbc.co.uk/radio4/news/anyquestions.shtml

G

Glossary

analyse (v) To break an issue down into parts in order to study, identify and discuss their meaning and/or relevance.

bias (n) An attitude you have, or a judgement you have made, based on subjective opinion instead of objective fact. It can make you treat someone or something in an unfair way.

common beliefs (n) Ideas that are accepted as true by many people even though there is no evidence for them.

concept (n) The characteristics or ideas associated with a class or group of objects. For example, the concept 'city' brings to mind traits common to all places classed as 'cities'. 'Paris' is not a concept as it refers to a single, specific place.

conclusion (n) The final part of a piece of academic writing, talk or presentation which sums up ideas and reaches a final result or judgement.

connotations (n) The set of associations implied by a word, in addition to its literal meaning.

counter-argument (n) An argument that opposes or makes the case against another argument.

critical thinking (n) The academic skill of being able to look at ideas and problems in a considered, critical way in order to evaluate them. It also involves the ability to see links between concepts and develop one's own ideas.

dissuade (v) Make someone stop believing an idea or argument, or prevent them from doing something, by reasoning with them.

downplay (n) Make something seem less important or significant in order to support our own ideas.

evaluate (v) To assess information in terms of quality, relevance, objectivity and accuracy.

fact (n) Something that is known or can be demonstrated to be true.

fallacy (n) A false belief that is due to faulty reasoning.

hyperbole (n) Huge overstatement which may be used to persuade someone of a viewpoint.

manipulate (v) To influence or control someone else's opinion in a dishonest way.

objective (adj) (n) 1 (adj) Not influenced by personal feelings or emotions. 2 (n) The aim, or what you want to achieve from an activity.

opinion (n) A personal belief that may be subjective and is not based on certainty or fact.

overstate (v) To exaggerate or state in terms that are stronger than necessary.

paraphrase (v) To alter a piece of text so that you restate it (concisely) in different words without changing its meaning. It is useful to paraphrase when writing a summary of someone's ideas; if the source is acknowledged, it is not plagiarism. It is also possible to paraphrase your own ideas in an essay or presentation; that is, to state them again, often in a clearer, expanded way.

peer pressure (n) The pressure on someone to conform and look, behave or think in the same way as other people.

persuade (v) Make someone believe something (such as an idea or argument) or do something, by reasoning with them.

poor argumentation (n) An argument that is not strong or sound because the conclusion does not follow from the premises, or because the premise is faulty.

premise (n) A statement that is assumed to be true by an author or speaker who is presenting an argument.

reasoning (n) The arguments or logic one uses to form conclusions and judgements.

sound argument (n) An argument where the conclusion absolutely follows from true premises. For example: All cats are carnivores: tigers are cats; therefore, tigers are carnivores. A sound argument is deductive (working from general to particular).

strategy (n) A plan of action that you follow when you want to achieve a particular goal. For example, it is possible to have a clear strategy for passing an exam.

strong argument (n) An argument where the conclusion does not necessarily follow from the premises, but if the premises are strong enough the conclusion is likely to be true. For example: Tigers sometimes eat people; therefore, this tiger is likely to eat us. A strong argument is inductive (working from particular to general).

subjective (adj) Describes an idea or opinion that is based on someone's personal opinion rather than on observable phenomena.

valid argument (n) An argument where the conclusion absolutely follows from the premises, but the premises may not be true. For example: All birds can fly; penguins are birds; therefore, penguins can fly.

vested interests (n) Seeking to maintain an existing system from which you get a personal benefit.

viewpoint (n) The mental position that someone sees things from. For example, the viewpoint of a child is different to that of its parent.

weak argument (n) An argument which is not valid, strong or sound because the premises are wrong and/or the conclusion does not follow from the premises.

Notes

Notes

Notes

Published by
Garnet Publishing Ltd
8 Southern Court
South Street
Reading RG1 4QS, UK

First published 2015.
Reprinted 2017.

ISBN 978-1-78260-178-4

British Library Cataloguing-in-Publication Data
A catalogue record for this book is available from the British Library.

Production

Project Manager:	Sophia Hopton
Editorial team:	Clare Chandler, Sophia Hopton, Martin Moore
Design & Layout:	Madeleine Maddock
Photography:	Corbis, iStockphoto, Shutterstock

Garnet Publishing and the authors of TASK would like to thank the staff and students of the International Foundation Programme at the University of Reading for their respective roles in the development of these teaching materials.

Garnet Publishing would like to thank Jane Brooks for her contribution to the First edition of the TASK series.

All website URLs provided in this publication were correct at the time of printing. If any URL does not work, please contact your tutor, who will help you find similar resources.

Printed and bound in Lebanon by International Press: interpress@int-press.com

Acknowledgements

Page 15: Task 1.2, *cheapskate* definition, Longman Dictionary of Contemporary English, Pearson Longman, Pearson Education Limited. Copyright © Pearson Longman 2014.

Page 23: Task 3.3, Cocacolonization article sourced from Wikipedia, http://en.wikipedia.org/wiki/Cocacolonization. Text has been modified and used under the CC-BA-SA 3.0 license, http://creativecommons.org/licenses/by-sa/3.0/legalcode.